RELIGIOUS LIVES

Moses and Judaism

Ruth Nason

WAYLAND

Religious Lives

The Buddha and Buddhism
Guru Nanak and Sikhism
Krishna and Hinduism

Krishna and Hinduism
Moses and Judaism
Muhammad and Islam

For more information on this series and other Wayland titles, go to www.waylandbooks.co.uk

© White-Thomson Publishing Ltd 2006

Produced for Hodder Wayland by White-Thomson Publishing Ltd
Bridgewater Business Centre, 210 High Street, Lewes, East Sussex BN7 2NH, UK

First published in 2006 by Hodder Wayland, an imprint of Hodder Children's Books
This paperback edition published in 2008 by Wayland, an imprint of Hachette Children's Books

This book is adapted from *Moses and Judaism* (*Great Religious Leaders* series) by Sharon Barron, published by Hodder Wayland in 2002

All rights reserved.

British Library Cataloguing in Publication Data
Nason, Ruth
Moses and Judaism, - Adapted Ed. - (Religious Lives)
1. Moses (Biblical leader) - Juvenile literature 2. Judaism - Juvenile literature
I. Title II.Barron, Sharon
222.1 '092

ISBN 978 0 7502 4796 2

Printed in China

Wayland
338 Euston Road, London NW1 3BH

Wayland is a division of Hachette Children's Books, an Hachette Livre UK Company
www.hachettelivre.co.uk

Title page: Orthodox Jews at a *Bar mitzvah* at the Western Wall, Jerusalem.

Picture Acknowledgements: The publisher would like to thank the following for permission to reproduce their pictures:
AKG 7 (Erich Lessing), 8 (Cameraphoto), 9, 10, 11 both, 12, 13, 14, 15, 16, 18, 22, 23, 33, Art Directors and Trip Photo Library 5 (A Tovy), 26 (H Rogers), 27 (top) (H Rogers), 27 bottom (I Genut), 30 (I Genut), 31 (J Greenberg), 32 (K McLaren), 36 (top) (J Greenberg), 36 (bottom) (I Genut), 43 (A Tovy), 45 (A Tovy); James Davis Photography 29; Paul Doyle title page; Eye Ubiquitous 20 (David Peez), 42 (Chris Fairclough); Sonia Halliday 34 (David Silverman), 38 (both) (David Silverman), 29 (David Silverman); Impact 24 (Rachel Morton), 28 (Simon Shepheard); Christine Osborne 7 (top), 19 (Ann Cook), 25, 40; Panos Pictures 44 (N. Durrell-McKenna); David Silverman 35, 41; Stockmarket 37, 40; Hodder Wayland Picture Library 6, 17 (Rupert Horrox).

Graphics and maps: Tim Mayer.

Contents

1. What is Judaism?   4
2. The Life of Moses   6
3. Moses the Leader and his Teaching   14
4. The Sacred Texts   20
5. Sacred and Special Places   28
6. Special Occasions and Festivals   34
7. Judaism Today   44

Glossary   46
Further Information   47
Index   48

What is Judaism?

Judaism is the religion of Jewish people. The story of how the religion began is told in the first five books of the Bible.

The beginning of Judaism

About 4,000 years ago people worshipped many gods, but a man called Abraham believed that there was only one God. Abraham heard God telling him to leave his home and go to a place called Canaan. God promised that Abraham's descendants would hold the land of Canaan for ever. They would be God's people. Because of God's promise to Abraham, Canaan became known as the 'Promised Land'.

▼ The land of Canaan was in roughly the same area as the present-day country of Israel.

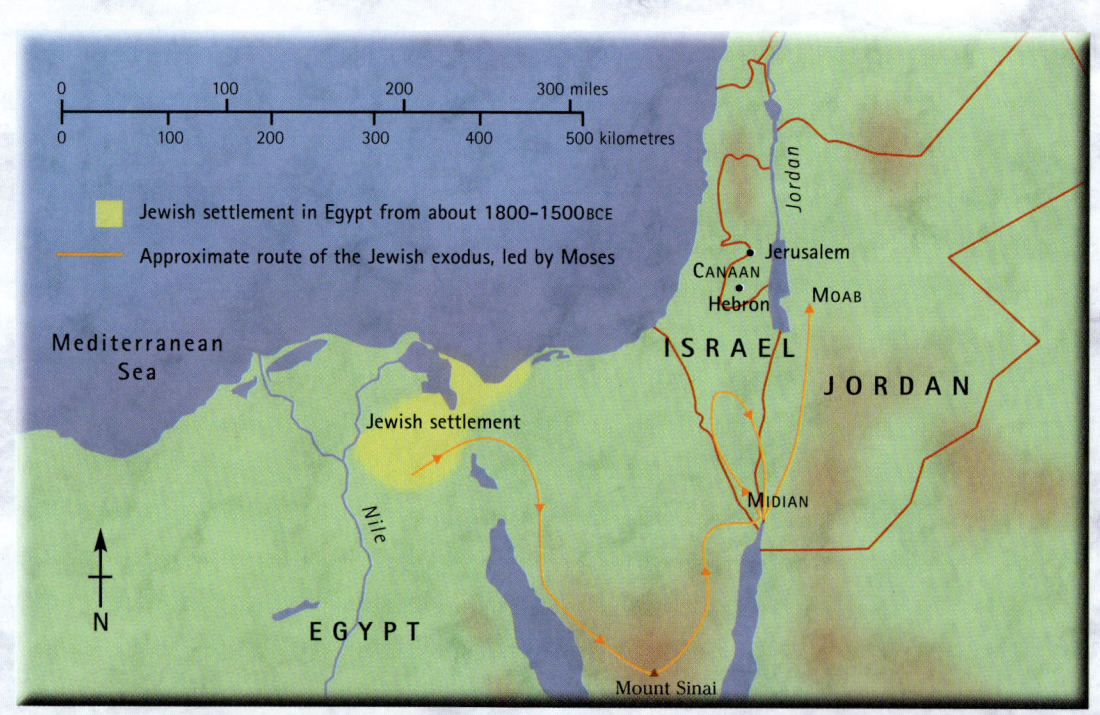

A traditional Jewish family at the Western Wall in Jerusalem (see page 30).

In the Bible Abraham and his descendants are called Hebrews and, later, Israelites. They stayed in Canaan for about 200 years. Then there was a terrible famine and they moved to Egypt. After a while, an Egyptian ruler, called a pharaoh, made them slaves.

Two hundred years later God helped a man called Moses to lead the people to freedom. God also gave Moses rules for the people to follow.

What do Jews believe?

Jews believe that there is one all-powerful God who is the creator of the universe. They believe that they are the descendants of Abraham and the Israelites. They must love God and follow the rules that God gave to Moses.

The Shema

An important passage from the Bible is called the *Shema*. It begins:

Hear, O Israel!
The LORD is our God, the LORD is one. You shall love the LORD your God with all your heart and with all your soul and with all your might.

(Deuteronomy 6: 4)

The Life of Moses

Slaves in Egypt

The Egyptian Pharaoh thought that there were too many Israelites in his country. He was worried that they might make trouble for him and so he made them work as slaves. They were treated cruelly.

Then the Pharaoh ordered that all Israelite baby boys should be killed as soon as they were born. He told the Egyptians to look for Israelite baby boys and throw them into the River Nile.

The baby Moses

One Israelite mother was determined to save her baby son. When he was three months old, she found a basket and covered it with tar to make it watertight. She put her baby into the basket and hid it in some reeds by the riverbank. She sent her daughter, Miriam, to watch over the baby from a distance.

▲ The Israelites were treated harshly as slaves in Egypt.

The basket was found by the Pharaoh's daughter. She realized that the baby inside was Israelite, but she did not want to harm him.

Miriam went nervously to her and said, 'If you are going to keep this baby, I could find you a good nurse.' The Egyptian princess adopted the baby, and his real mother became his nurse.

▶ The baby was drawn out of the river. The princess called him Moses, a name which came from words that mean 'draw out'.

The Egyptian princess

The princess must have been very brave to go against the orders of the Pharaoh, her father. The Bible gives her name as Bithia. This means 'Daughter of God'.

▲ This ancient Egyptian painting shows how the princess might have looked.

The burning bush

Moses became a prince of Egypt. Then one day he saw an Egyptian man beating an Israelite slave. This made Moses so angry that he killed the Egyptian.

The Egyptians wanted to punish Moses for this and so he fled to Midian, outside Egypt. There he saw some men attacking some girls who were looking after a flock of sheep. Moses rescued the girls and their family welcomed him. He married one of the girls and became a shepherd in Midian. He was happy in his new life.

One day, while out with the sheep, Moses saw an incredible sight: a bush was burning but staying undamaged. A voice called to Moses from the bush, saying it was the voice of God.

God told Moses to return to Egypt. He must tell the Pharaoh to free the slaves, and he must tell the Israelites that he would lead them out of Egypt and into the Promised Land.

▲ This ancient mosaic shows Moses and the burning bush.

The Life of Moses

Moses said, 'No one will listen to me. Pharaoh won't let the slaves go and they won't believe what I say!'

God said that he would make things happen to show that Moses must be believed. For example, the shepherd's crook that Moses held could be changed into a snake.

Moses said, 'But I get nervous and stutter when I speak to people.'

God replied, 'Don't protest any more. I will send your brother, Aaron, with you as your spokesperson.'

▲ These illustrations of the story of Moses come from a special Jewish book called a *Hagadah* (see page 41).

A legend about Moses

Moses was chasing after a stray lamb and at last it stopped to drink from a stream. Moses was sorry that he had not realized the lamb was thirsty. He carried it all the way back to the flock. When God noticed how Moses cared for one stray lamb, he chose him to lead and look after the Israelites, God's people.

Let my people go!

When Moses and Aaron first asked the Pharaoh to set the slaves free, he just laughed and made the slaves work even harder. The Pharaoh was not impressed when the shepherd's crook was changed into a snake. Then Aaron held the crook over the River Nile and the water turned to blood. But the Pharaoh's own magicians did the same tricks.

▲ These pictures in a *Hagadah* show the plagues. The Hebrew language is written from right to left, so the first plague is at the top right.

The Life of Moses

◀ Before the tenth plague, God told the Israelites to kill a lamb to eat and put its blood on their doorposts. The Angel of Death would pass over their homes. Only Egyptians would die.

Turning the river to blood was the first of ten plagues that God sent to Egypt. The Egyptian people begged the Pharaoh to free the slaves so that the plagues would stop, but the Pharaoh would not give in. There were plagues of frogs, lice and flies. A disease killed all the Egyptians' animals. Then people became ill with boils. A hailstorm ruined the crops, locusts ate the crops, and there was darkness for three days and nights.

In the tenth plague, the first-born sons in every Egyptian family were killed. At last the Pharaoh said that the slaves could leave.

God had told the Israelites to be ready to leave quickly. When they reached the Sea of Reeds they realized that Egyptian soldiers had chased after them. However, God told Moses to hold his arm out over the sea. Miraculously, the water moved apart, making a dry way across for the Israelites. The Egyptians tried to follow but the sea returned to normal and they were all drowned.

In the desert

Moses and the Israelites travelled on into the desert and, after seven weeks, they arrived at Mount Sinai. God called Moses up the mountain to receive God's laws for the people. Moses stayed there for forty days and nights.

While he was away, the Israelites grew restless. They thought he would not come back. Aaron had been left in charge of them and he told them to collect together all the gold jewellery that they could find. This was melted down and moulded into a golden statue of a calf.

Soon the people forgot about God and Moses. They decided to believe that the statue of the golden calf had rescued them from Egypt. They worshipped the statue instead of God.

▼ The golden calf was something that the Israelites could see to worship.

God told Moses that he would destroy the Israelites for this, but Moses pleaded for them. He returned to the people with God's laws written on tablets of stone.

When Moses saw the golden statue he was so angry that he threw the tablets of stone on the ground. He broke the statue, ground the pieces into powder, mixed them with water and made the Israelites drink it. Some people had not worshipped the calf statue. Moses ordered them to kill everyone who had.

▲ About 3,000 people were killed for forgetting God and worshipping the golden calf.

Aaron

Aaron was Moses' elder brother. He has become known as a peace-loving man and this may be why he gave in to the people and built the golden calf. Perhaps he believed that making a statue to worship would calm the people and stop them from fighting each other.

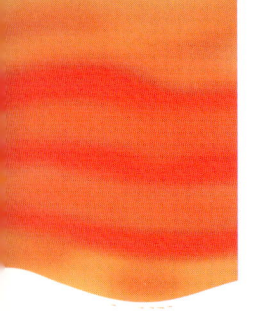

Moses the Leader and his Teaching

We know that Moses was brought up as an Egyptian prince, but he was a humble man. He had a stutter and felt nervous about speaking to people. He helped people when he saw them being badly treated. He was a caring shepherd.

▲ Moses strikes the rock and water gushes from it.

Sometimes Moses lost his temper. When the Israelites were in the desert, they grumbled because they needed water. God told Moses to gather the people together by a rock and to ask the rock for water. Moses was anxious and angry and he hit the rock twice with his crook.

Water gushed out, but Moses had disobeyed God. By hitting the rock, he made it look as though he himself had caused the water to appear. Moses should have shown that the water came from God.

The Bible says that when he came down from Mount Sinai, Moses looked 'radiant' (shining). But once the word for 'radiant' was wrongly translated as 'with horns'. This explains why some old illustrations show Moses with horns.

Several times Moses questioned what God said. When God told him to speak to the Pharaoh, Moses argued that he could not do it. When God said he would destroy the Israelites for building the golden calf, Moses begged him not to.

How do Jewish people regard Moses?

Moses is very special to Jewish people. They respect him because he was chosen by God to help the Israelites, their ancestors. Jewish people call Moses 'our teacher' because he taught people God's laws.

Never again did there arise in Israel a prophet like Moses – whom the Lord singled out, face to face, for the various signs ... that the Lord sent him to display ...

(Deuteronomy 34: 10)

The Bible describes how Moses received God's laws, written on stone tablets.

Moses the prophet

Jewish people believe that Moses was a prophet. A prophet was someone chosen by God to give the people God's message, to tell them when they were doing wrong and to show them the right way to behave.

There were many other important prophets and the Bible includes the stories of them all. Jewish people believe that Moses was the most special prophet in God's eyes.

The covenant

A covenant is a two-sided agreement. Jewish people believe that God made a covenant with Moses, the Israelites and their descendants. One side of the covenant was that God promised always to take care of the people. The other side of the covenant was that the people promised always to keep the laws that God gave to Moses.

Moses the Leader and his Teaching 17

► One of God's laws for the Jewish people is to keep one day of the week holy. On this day, called *Shabbat*, many Jewish people go to the synagogue.

Jewish people believe that this covenant continues forever, between them and God.

Sometimes Jewish people are described as God's 'Chosen People'. They believe that God chose them because they were willing to follow God's laws.

Now then, if you will obey Me faithfully and keep My covenant, you shall be My treasured possession among all the peoples …
(Exodus 19: 5–6)

God's commandments

While the Israelites were in the desert, after escaping from Egypt, God called Moses to the top of Mount Sinai. Here God gave Moses rules or laws that the people must always follow. These rules are often called 'commandments' and the main ones are known as the Ten Commandments.

The first four of the Ten Commandments are about how people must worship only God. They include the commandment to keep one day of the week holy and not do any work on that day (see *Shabbat*, pages 34-35).

How to treat others

The fifth to the tenth of the Ten Commandments are about how people must treat each other. They are:
  5. Honour your parents.
  6. Do not murder.
  7. Do not commit adultery.
  8. Do not steal.
  9. Do not say untrue things about each other.
  10. Do not want things that belong to others.

(Exodus 20: 12–17)

▲ The Bible story tells that God came to Moses in a thick cloud.

Hasidic Jews are one particular group of Orthodox Jews. They still dress in the same way as the first Hasidic Jews, who lived in Poland in the eighteenth century.

Mitzvot

The Hebrew word for 'commandments' is *mitzvot* and there are 613 of them altogether.

There are many *mitzvot* about food. Food that Jewish people are allowed to eat is called *kosher*. Another group of *mitzvot* deals with helping people in need.

Today, Orthodox Jews follow the *mitzvot* exactly as they are written. They believe that doing this will bring them closer to God. They believe that the *mitzvot* must not be altered.

Other Jewish people think that the *mitzvot* can be adapted to a modern way of life.

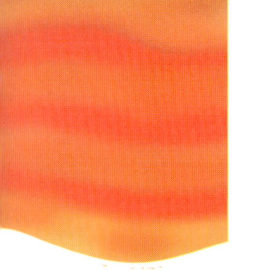

The Sacred Texts

The Jewish Bible was written in Hebrew, the language of the Israelites. It has three parts, each made up of several books. The first part is the *Torah*.

The Torah

Five books make up the *Torah*. The first, called Genesis, begins with God creating the world. It also tells how Abraham heard God's promise that he and his descendants would be 'God's people' (see page 4).

The other four books are about Moses. They contain the laws that God gave to Moses to teach to the Israelites. This explains why this part of the Bible is called the *Torah*, the Hebrew word for 'Law'.

◀ These men are carrying a *Torah* scroll in a beautifully decorated cover.

The *Torah* is the most precious part of the Bible for Jewish people and they show great respect for it. The *Torah* is written on a scroll (see page 26) and the scroll is kept in a beautiful cover.

The Torah and the Christian Bible

The five books which make up the *Torah* are also the first five books of the Christian Bible.

▼ This father is helping his son to learn to read the *Torah*. They are using a printed book which includes an English translation as well as the words in Hebrew.

Reading the Torah

A reading from the *Torah* is an important part of services at the synagogue. The *Torah* has been divided into 54 sections and, starting from the beginning, one section is read each week. In a year the whole of the *Torah* is read. In the week when the last section is read, the first section is read too, and people celebrate with a festival called *Simchat Torah* (see page 43).

Nevi'im

Nevi'im means 'Prophets' (see page 16). The books in this part of the Jewish Bible tell what happened to the Israelites after Moses died. First Joshua led the people into Canaan, the Promised Land. In their new country the people were ruled by kings including Saul, David and Solomon. After King Solomon died, the country was divided into two kingdoms, Judah and Israel. In different situations, prophets tried to make the people remember God.

▲ Before Moses died, God told him to find Joshua and place his hand on him. This showed that he was passing on the leadership of the Israelites to Joshua.

The Sacred Texts

At services in the synagague, the *Torah* reading (see page 21) is followed by a reading from the *Nevi'im*.

Ketuvim

Ketuvim means 'writings'. The first book in this part of the Jewish Bible is the Book of Psalms, 150 songs praising God. It is thought that many of them could have been written by King David. Psalms are an important part of synagogue services.

The Tenakh

Another name for the Jewish Bible is the *Tenakh*. It is made from the first letters of the *Torah*, *Nevi'im* and *Ketuvim* – TNK.

▼ In the Bible story, Jonah is swallowed by a big fish, but when people tell the story they usually say that he was swallowed by a whale.

The story of Jonah

The Bible tells how God chose prophets to speak to the people for God. When God called Jonah to be a prophet, Jonah ran away because he thought it was too difficult. The story tells that he was caught in a storm at sea, thrown overboard and swallowed by a big fish. Eventually he came safely to the shore and went to speak to the people in Nineveh, as God had told him.

The writings of the rabbis

People who taught the Jews about the *Torah* were called 'rabbi' – 'my master' or 'my teacher'. Some writings by *rabbis* from long ago are the *Talmud* and the *Midrash*.

The *Talmud* was written between 200 and 500 CE. It is a record of the studies of many of the first *rabbis*. They discussed how God's laws in the *Torah* should be followed.

▼ This woman *rabbi* is using a pointer called a *yad* to follow the words in a *Torah* scroll.

Rabbis today

Rabbis today still spend a lot of time teaching and explaining Jewish law. They may lead services in the synagogue, but this can also be done by a member of the congregation. Women can become *rabbis* of non-Orthodox communities, but there are no women *rabbis* in Orthodox Judaism.

The *Midrash* is a collection of writings by *rabbis*, which explain and explore parts of the Bible. Nearly all these writings are in the form of a story. A famous one explains how Moses got his stutter.

The story is that, once, when Moses was a boy, the Pharaoh showed him a precious jewel and a pan of hot coals. The Pharaoh's advisers had said, 'If Moses takes the jewel, he will one day try to take your throne.' So, if Moses took the jewel, the Pharaoh meant to kill him.

Moses started to reach for the jewel, but an angel nudged his hand towards the coals. Moses picked up a hot coal, touched his mouth and burnt his lips and tongue. This gave him his stutter.

▲ Studying together is important in Judaism. Even in the Second World War, when Jewish people suffered persecution, these Jews in Poland gathered together to study.

The *Torah* scrolls inside this Ark have velvet covers. Silver ornaments and *yads* hang around them.

The Torah scrolls

A scroll in which the *Torah* is written is called a *Sefer Torah*. The scrolls are kept in a special cupboard in the synagogue called the Ark. Beautiful covers are made for them. At services everyone stands up when a *Sefer Torah* is taken from the Ark.

A *Torah* scroll is made from pieces of parchment sewn together to make a length of 60 metres. Wooden poles are attached, one to each end. The two poles are used to unwind the scroll as it is read.

It may take a year to write a *Torah* scroll. The words are carefully handwritten in 250 columns. When a *Torah* scroll becomes old, the writing fades. When it can no longer be read, the scroll is buried with great respect.

The Shema

The passage from the *Torah* called the *Shema* (see page 5) says that Jews must always think of God's commandments. It says 'tie them on your hands and foreheads' and 'write them on your door frames'. This is why some Jewish people strap little boxes called *tefillin* to their forehead and left arm, and why many Jewish people have a little box called a *mezuzah* fixed by their front door. Inside the *tefillin* and the *mezuzah* is a tiny scroll with the words of the *Shema* on it.

▲ The small piece of parchment is rolled up and put inside the little case.

▼ Orthodox Jewish men put on *tefillin* to say their morning prayers.

Sacred and Special Places

The only Jewish country in the world is Israel, which was founded in 1948. It is in the area of the Middle East that Jews believe God promised to Abraham and his descendants 4,000 years ago.

▲ Many kinds of fruit are grown in Israel.

The name 'Israel'

The *Torah* includes the story of Jacob, one of Abraham's grandsons. He became known as 'Israel', which means 'struggles with God' and so the people became known as Israelites. The land of Canaan, which God had promised to them, became known as the land of Israel.

Joshua led the Israelites into this 'Promised Land' (see page 22), but later they were forced out. They went to live in many other places but always remembered the 'Promised Land' and wanted to return. Today Jewish people everywhere still think of Israel as their special homeland.

Jerusalem

Jerusalem is the capital city of modern Israel. It was also the capital in the time of King David (see page 22) about 3,000 years ago. It is sometimes called the 'City of David'. David's son, King Solomon, built a temple there.

After 300 years people from Babylon attacked the city, forced the Jewish people out and destroyed the temple. Eventually the Jews returned and another temple was built. Then in 70 CE this temple was destroyed by the ancient Romans.

Jerusalem is very important for Jewish people, and also for Christians and Muslims. People from all these religions visit Jerusalem.

▼ This view of Jerusalem shows the Western Wall, which is important to Jews; the Dome of the Rock, which is important to Muslims; and a Russian Christian church.

The Western Wall

The most sacred Jewish site in Jerusalem is the Western Wall. It is a wall that was built around the first and second temples. Jewish people go to the Western Wall to express their sadness that the temples were destroyed. Sometimes it is called the Wailing Wall.

Visitors often write prayers on pieces of paper and push them into the gaps between the stones of the Wall. Many young Jewish people have their *Bar mitzvah* and *Bat mitzvah* ceremonies (see pages 36-37) in the area in front of the Wall.

▼ These boys are visiting the Western Wall, to prepare for their *Bar mitzvah*.

Jewish people place a small stone on a grave, as a sign that they have visited.

Burial places

The oldest and largest Jewish cemetery is on the Mount of Olives in Jerusalem. Jews have been buried there for more than 2,000 years.

Pilgrims visit the tomb of King David in Jerusalem, although it is probably not his real burial place. They also go to the Cave of Machpelah in Hebron, where Abraham, Isaac and Jacob, the Patriarchs or 'fathers' of the Jewish people, are thought to be buried.

Jewish people pray to God at these famous burial places and at the graves of famous *rabbis*. Sometimes they leave written prayers there.

The death of Moses

There is a legend that, as Moses died, he was kissed by God.

He buried him in the valley of the land of Moab ... and no one knows his burial place to this day.

(Deuteronomy 34: 5–60)

The Holocaust

At the time of the Second World War the Nazi rulers of Germany wanted to destroy all Jewish people. They sent Jews from all over Europe to death camps. Six million Jews were killed – one third of all Jews in the world. This destruction of the Jewish people was called the Holocaust or the *Shoah*.

◀ This is the Children's Memorial at Yad Vashem.

Places to remember the Holocaust

Around the world there are memorials to people who died in the Holocaust.

Yad Vashem is the memorial in Jerusalem. Visitors can see exhibitions, art and information about the Holocaust. There is a display of the names of all the people who died and a special memorial to the 1.5 million children who were killed.

In many countries Holocaust museums have been opened in memory of the people who died. One famous museum is the Anne Frank House in Amsterdam, Holland.

The story of Anne Frank

Anne Frank was a schoolgirl in Amsterdam at the time of the Second World War. Her family was Jewish and so they were in great danger when the Nazis invaded Holland.

Her father found them a secret hiding place above his office, and they stayed safe there for two years. Then they were captured and sent to a death camp. Anne died two months before the war ended.

Anne's father, Otto Frank, survived and when he returned to Amsterdam he found Anne's diary, which she had written while in hiding. The diary was published and Anne became famous. Today her hiding place is a museum and thousands of people visit from all over the world.

▲ Anne Frank and seven other people hid in a place called the Secret Annexe. The diary that Anne wrote there has now been published in more than 50 languages.

Special Occasions and Festivals

As well as festivals that happen once each year, Jewish people celebrate one special day every week. It begins on Friday evening and is called *Shabbat*.

Shabbat

Jewish people keep this day special because of God's commandment to keep one day of the week holy (see page 18). The commandment says that people should not do any work on this day.

Shabbat is a family time. To begin *Shabbat*, the woman of the house lights two candles and says a blessing. If there are children, the father blesses them, placing his hands over their heads.

Other blessings are recited over a cup of wine and over two loaves of bread called *challah*. Then the family enjoys a special meal together.

◀ The woman says a blessing over the two *Shabbat* candles.

Even Jewish families who are not religious keep the custom of gathering together for a special meal on Friday evening.

On Saturday mornings many families attend a service at the synagogue. Orthodox Jews follow the commandment strictly and do not do anything on *Shabbat* that could be called work. This includes switching on electricity and driving a car.

Challah

Challah is a type of plaited bread. Two loaves are needed for *Shabbat*. They remind Jews of the food, called manna, that God gave to the Israelites in the desert (see page 12). On the sixth day of the week, God sent them enough manna for two days. This meant that they did not need to collect food on the seventh day and could keep the day holy.

▶ Children take part in the *Shabbat* meal.

▲ This young man is being carried on his father's shoulders after his *Bar mitzvah* at the Western Wall in Jerusalem.

▼ This young man is making a speech at the party to celebrate his *Bar mitzvah*.

Bar mitzvah

To mark the time when a Jewish boy becomes a man, old enough to follow all the Jewish laws, there is a ceremony called *Bar mitzvah*. This means 'son of the commandment'. The ceremony usually takes place on the *Shabbat* after the boy's 13th birthday.

At the synagogue service on that day the *Bar mitzvah* boy reads aloud from the *Torah* scroll. This is an important time and the boy works hard beforehand to learn how to do the reading.

Afterwards there is a party for the boy. His parents and grandparents give him presents that he will keep always, such as a prayer shawl or *tefillin* (see page 27).

Bat mitzvah

Jewish girls are considered to reach adulthood at the age of 12 but until recently there was no special ceremony to mark this time. Nowadays many Jewish girls do have a *Bat mitzvah* ceremony. *Bat mitzvah* means 'daughter of the commandment'.

Before her *Bat mitzvah* ceremony, a girl learns about the commandments called *mitzvot* (see page 19) and about Jewish history. She also learns how to run a Jewish home.

The ceremonies vary. There is not really a set form. In non-Orthodox branches of Judaism *Bat mitzvah* ceremonies take place, like *Bar mitzvah* ones, in the *Shabbat* morning service.

▲ This girl is reading from the *Torah* scroll at her *Bat mitzvah* ceremony in a non-Orthodox synagogue.

Preparing for Pesach

Pesach is also called Passover. This festival takes place in spring and lasts for eight days. It is a time to remember how God helped the Israelites to escape from slavery in Egypt, led by Moses (see pages 10-11).

On the night that the Israelites left Egypt, they made bread for their journey. They had to leave quickly and there was not time to let the bread dough rise before it was cooked. The bread was flat. To remember this, during *Pesach*, Jewish people do not eat any foods made with yeast to make them rise. Instead of bread they eat *matzah*, which is like a cracker or crispbread.

▲ Foods that have been allowed to rise are called *hametz*. All such foods are burned before *Pesach*.

▶ *Matzah* dough is baked within 18 minutes so it has no time to rise.

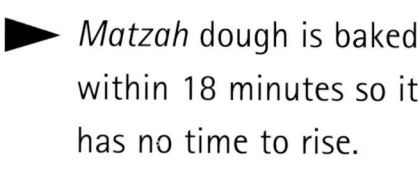

Special Occasions and Festivals

▶ Utensils are thoroughly washed so that no trace of *hametz* is left on them.

To prepare for the festival, every trace of *hametz* (food made with a raising agent like yeast) is removed from the house. The house is spring-cleaned and the usual crockery, cutlery and kitchen equipment are put away. Special sets, used only during *Pesach*, are brought out instead.

Jewish families all have their favourite foods for *Pesach*. There are many delicious recipes for special cakes and biscuits.

Searching for hametz

A custom on the evening before *Pesach* is for somebody to hide some pieces of bread around the house. Then everyone searches for them until all the pieces have been found. By doing this the family makes sure that they have made a thorough search of the house and no trace of *hametz* (leavened food) remains.

Celebrating Pesach

On the first two nights of *Pesach* Jewish families gather at home for a service called the *Seder*. Often they invite others to join them so that no one is alone for this part of the festival.

Seder means 'order' and at the service everything is done in a set order. The service is divided into two parts by a special meal and everyone in the family is involved.

▼ Three pieces of *matzah* are placed on the *Seder* table. One is broken in two and half is used for the *Afikomen* (see page 41).

▲ This illustration from a *Hagadah* goes with a song called 'One Kid'.

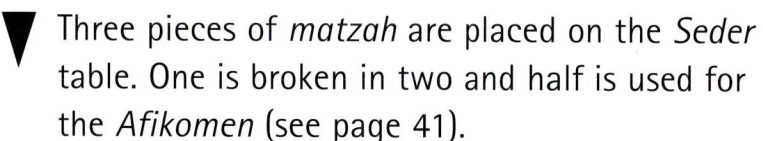

Special Occasions and Festivals

People follow the *Seder* service in a book called a *Hagadah*. The youngest child at the table asks four questions from the *Hagadah* about why the *Seder* night is different from all other nights. The answers tell how Moses was sent by God to lead the Israelites out of slavery in Egypt.

On the table there is a *Seder* plate with sections for particular foods. These foods help to tell the story of the Israelites. Everyone tastes the *haroset* (a mixture of apples, nuts, cinnamon and sugar). It is meant to be like the mortar that the Israelite slaves used in building. Everyone also tastes the bitter herbs, which represent the bitterness of slavery.

The *Seder* takes Jews back to a time when they suffered greatly, but by the end they look forward to a time when everyone will enjoy peace and freedom. The *Seder* ends with the words, 'Next year in Jerusalem!'

▲ People take turns to read aloud from the *Hagadah*.

The Afikomen

During the *Seder* evening a father hides the half piece of *matzah* called the *Afikomen* (see page 40). After dinner the children hunt for it. The *Seder* cannot end until the *Afikomen* has been found and eaten. The finder gets a reward, as do all the other children who joined in the search.

Shavuot

Seven weeks after *Pesach* there is the festival of *Shavuot*. It lasts for two days and is a time to remember Moses receiving God's laws. The Ten Commandments are read at a service in the synagogue.

For the festival of *Sukkot* people build a temporary shelter. Its roof is made from branches and left partly open to the sky.

Sukkot

At *Sukkot* people think of the Israelites who lived in the desert for forty years after escaping from Egypt. God protected them and gave them food.

For this festival, many families build a shelter outdoors, called a *sukkah*. This reminds them of the shelters that the Israelites built in the desert. For the eight days of the festival the family eat all their meals and sometimes sleep in the *sukkah*.

The name of the festival, *Sukkot*, means 'shelters'.

The four species

Four types of plant called 'the four species' are used when Jews pray at *Sukkot*. The four plants are: palm, myrtle, willow and an etrog – a yellow fruit rather like a lemon.

Every day of the festival the four plants are held together and waved in all directions. This is a symbol of God showering His blessings everywhere.

▲ People try hard to find the freshest and most perfect plants to use for 'the four species'.

Simchat Torah

The eighth day of *Sukkot* is called *Simchat Torah*. At this festival Jewish people show their love for God's laws in the *Torah*. This is the day of the year when the last section and the first section of the *Torah* are read in the synagogue (see page 21). The *Torah* scroll is carried in a joyful parade around the synagogue, and sometimes outdoors.

Judaism Today

There are about 15 million Jewish people today. The largest numbers are in the United States and in Israel. Israel has a 'Law of Return', which gives every Jew in the world the right to go and live there and become an Israeli citizen.

▲ In the late twentieth century, when Jews in Ethiopia were persecuted, they were rescued and taken to live in Israel.

Different groups

Jewish people come from different racial groups, which have their own customs. The two main groups are Ashkenazi (from Northern, Central and Eastern Europe) and Sephardi (from Spain, Portugal and the Arab countries). There are also Oriental Jews (for example from India and Yemen) and Jews from Ethiopia.

Orthodox and non-Orthodox

Some Jewish people no longer practise their religion. Jewish people who do follow the religious practices are called 'observant Jews' and belong either to the Orthodox branch of the religion or to the non-Orthodox branch.

Orthodox Jews follow traditional religious rules and customs. They believe that God's laws in the *Torah* can never be changed. Some Orthodox Jews belong to Hasidic groups, who follow the traditions very strictly.

Non-Orthodox Jews believe that the religion can be adapted for the changing, modern world. There are several different groups of non-Orthodox Jews. They may be called Reform, Liberal or Progressive.

However, all observant Jews, both Orthodox and non-Orthodox, believe that the *Torah* is the 'heart' of their religion. It has shaped the lives of all Jewish people to this day. Therefore Moses, who received the law for the people and led them towards their 'Promised Land', has a very special place in Judaism indeed.

▼ Following the Orthodox tradition for men and women to worship separately, the area near the Western Wall in Jerusalem is divided into a men's and a women's section.

Glossary

angel a heavenly being, believed to be sent by God to do or say something.

Bible one of the holy books of the Jewish people, also known as the *Tenakh*. The Jewish Bible is very similar to the part of the Christian Bible that is called the Old Testament. For Jewish people, the first five books of the Bible are the most important. They are known as the *Torah* (Law).

bless to wish deep happiness on someone, in the belief that this happiness comes from God.

blessing a short prayer.

congregation all the people who meet for worship in a particular place.

Hagadah a book used at the festival of *Pesach*. It allows everyone to take part in the *Seder* service and meal, remembering how the Israelites were slaves in Egypt and how they escaped, led by Moses.

Hebrews a name used for the first Jewish people, from the time of Abraham. They spoke the Hebrew language, which is the language of the *Torah* and of Jewish prayers. A modern version of Hebrew is the everyday language of Israel today.

holy set apart for God.

Israelites a name used for the Jewish people since Jacob, a grandson of Abraham, was given the name 'Israel' by God. The Jewish people are also referred to as the 'Children of Israel' and sometimes simply as 'Israel'.

kosher right to eat, according to the Jewish food laws called *kashrut*.

Orthodox keeping the religion according to the law. Orthodox Jews believe that the law in the *Torah* cannot be changed. Non-Orthodox Jews believe that the law can be adapted to modern life.

Passover another name for the festival of *Pesach*. The name comes from the story of the tenth plague when the Angel of Death 'passed over' the Israelites' houses. Only Egyptians died.

Patriarch a male head of a family. Abraham, Isaac, Jacob and Jacob's twelve sons are the Patriarchs of the Jewish people.

persecution suffering or death inflicted on people because of their religion or the group they belong to.

plague a dreadful happening, taken as a sign of God's anger.

prayer shawl a shawl worn by all Jewish men and by some Jewish women and boys at services in the synagogue. It is called a *tallit*.

rabbi a Jewish religious teacher who may preach at the synagogue.

service an act of worship wtih a set pattern.

Shoah the Hebrew word which Jewish people use for the Holocaust. It means 'whirlwind'.

synagogue a building where Jewish people go to meet, worship together and study.

Further Information

Books

21st Century Religions: Judaism by Michael Keene (Wayland, 2005)

A Year of Religious Festivals: My Jewish Year by Cath Senker (Wayland, 2002)

Celebrate!: Passover by Mike Hirst (Wayland, 2002)

Celebration Stories: The Taste of Winter by Adele Geras (Wayland, 2002)

Facts About Judaism by Alison Cooper (Wayland, 2005)

Festivals: Passover by Angela Wood (Wayland, 2000)

Festival Stories: The Hanukkah Story by Anita Ganeri (Evans Publishing, 2003)

Festival Stories: The Passover Story by Anita Ganeri (Evans Publishing, 2004)

Holy Cities: Jerusalem by Nicola Barber (Evans Publishing, 2003)

Storyteller: Jewish Stories by Anita Ganeri (Evans Publishing Group, 2000)

Visiting a Synagogue by Ruth Nason (Evans Publishing, 2004)

World of Festivals: Hanukkah by D. and G. Rose and A. Clark (Evans Publishing, 2003)

World Religions Today by Gianna Quaglia (Wayland, 2008)

Website

http://www.akhlah.com/
A site for Jewish children with information about the *Torah*, festivals, Israel and Hebrew.

Resources for teachers

http://www.reonline.org.uk
A 'family of websites' including some for teachers and some for pupils. Serves as a gateway to over 300 RE resources drawn from all over the web.

http://www.theredirectory.org.uk

http://www.jewfaq.org/
An online encyclopaedia of Judaism.

BBC Education produces schools media resources on different faiths. See:
http://www.bbc.co.uk/schools

Channel 4 produces schools media resources on different faiths, including *Animated World Faiths*. Download catalogue from:
http://www.channel4.com/learning

Museums

Jewish Museum, 4 Shakespeae Road, London N3 1XE
http://www.jewishmuseum.org.uk

Manchester Jewish Museum, 190 Cheetham Hill Road, Manchester M8 8LW
http://www.mancesterjewishmuseum.com

The Irish Jewish Museum, 3/4 Walworth Road, South Circular Road, Dublin 8
http://www.jewishireland.org/museum.html

Beth Shalom Holocaust Centre, Laxton, Newark, Nottinghamshire NG22 OPA
http://www.bethshalom.com

Index

Aaron 9, 10, 12, 13
Abraham 4, 5, 20, 28, 31
Afikomen 40, 41
Ark 26
Ashkenazi Jews 44

Babylon 29
Bar mitzvah 30, 36
Bar mitzvah 30, 37
Bible 4, 5, 7, 15, 16, 18, 20, 21, 22, 23, 25, 34
bread 35, 38
burning bush 8

Canaan 4, 5, 22, 28
challah 35
commandments 18, 19, 27, 36, 37
   Ten Commandments 18, 34, 42
covenant 16, 17

David (King) 22, 23, 28, 31

Egypt 4, 5, 6, 7, 8, 11, 12, 18, 35, 38, 41, 42, 45

food 19, 35, 39, 41, 42
four species 43
Frank, Anne 33

golden calf 12, 13, 15
graves 31

Hagadah 9, 10, 40–41
hametz 38, 39
Hasidic Jews 19, 45

Holocaust 32, 33

Israel 4, 22, 28, 44
Israelites 5, 6, 8, 9, 11, 12, 13, 15, 16, 20, 22, 28, 35, 38, 41, 42

Jacob 28, 31
Jerusalem 4, 28, 29, 41
   burial places 31
   temple 28, 29
   Western Wall 5, 29, 30, 36, 45
   Yad Vashem 32
Jonah 23
Joshua 22, 28

Ketuvim 20, 23
kosher food 19

laws from God 5, 12, 13, 15, 16, 17, 18, 24, 36, 42, 43, 45

matzah 38, 40, 41
mezuzah 27
Midrash 25
Miriam 6, 7
mitzvot 19, 37
Moses 5, 20, 38, 41, 42, 45
   as prophet 16
   baby 6-7
   death 22, 31
   in the desert 12, 13, 14, 18
   in Midian 8
   stutter 9, 14, 25

Nevi'im 20, 22, 23

non-Orthodox Jews 24, 37, 44, 45
Orthodox Jews 19, 24, 27, 35, 44, 45

Patriarchs 31
Pesach 38, 39, 40, 41, 42
Pharaoh 5, 6, 7, 8, 9, 10, 11, 15, 25
plagues 10, 11
Promised Land 4, 8, 22, 28, 45
prophets 15, 16, 22, 23
Psalms 23

rabbis 24, 25, 31

Saul (King) 22
Second World War 25, 32, 33
Seder 40, 41
Sephardi Jews 44
Shabbat 17, 18, 34, 35, 36, 37
Shavuot 42
Shema 5, 27
Simchat Torah 21, 43
Solomon (King) 22, 28
Sukkot 42, 43
synagogue 17, 21, 23, 24, 26, 35, 36, 37, 42, 43

Talmud 24
tefillin 27, 36
Tenakh 23
Torah 20, 21, 24, 26, 27, 28, 43, 45
Torah scrolls 20, 24, 26, 27, 36, 37, 43

Printed in Great Britain
by Amazon